THE CORNELL BREAD BOOK

54 Recipes for Nutritious Loaves, Rolls & Coffee Cakes

CLIVE M. McCAY
&
JEANETTE B. McCAY

Dover Publications, Inc.
New York

Published in Canada by General Publishing Company, Ltd., 30 Lesmill Road, Don Mills, Toronto, Ontario.
Published in the United Kingdom by Constable and Company, Ltd., 10 Orange Street, London WC2H 7EG.

This Dover edition, first published in 1980, is a revised and enlarged version of the booklet originally titled *You Can Make Cornell Bread* by Clive M. McCay and Jeanette B. McCay. Published by Jeanette B. McCay, Englewood, FL, in 1955, it was revised in 1961 and 1973.

International Standard Book Number: 0-486-23995-0
Library of Congress Catalog Card Number: 80-66137

Manufactured in the United States of America
Dover Publications, Inc.
180 Varick Street
New York, N.Y. 10014

Contents

Clive Maine McCay (1898–1967) with two of his experimental
subjects in his studies to lengthen life.

The Do-Good Loaf

In the 1930's, my late husband, Clive M. McCay, professor of Animal Nutrition at Cornell University, Ithaca, New York, started a series of studies to learn the effect of nutrition on the life span of fish, white rats and dogs. His experiments showed that by cutting down on calories but providing plenty of minerals, vitamins and protein in their diets, he could slow their growth and retard the onset of old-age diseases and death. The thin rats always buried the fat ones. His animals on the low-calorie diet often lived twice as long as those allowed to eat their fill.

During these laboratory studies, Clive concluded that the health of people could also be improved through diet. When asked to help the New York State Mental Hospitals make their food better, he chose to improve the quality of the bread, because the patients tended to eat more bread than average persons, and sometimes it was the only food they would eat. This, he felt, would bring the greatest benefit at the lowest cost.

With the help of the hospitals' dieticians, their bakers, and a specialist from the Dry Milk Institute, the high-protein "Cornell formula" was developed.

Its recipe went from hospitals to school lunch programs, commercial bakeries, home bureaus, and home bakers all over the United States. The experience of World War II contributed to the interest in it and its spread, due to meat rationing and the need to find other sources of protein. It was a time like the present, when the meat dollar doesn't go far enough.

The original booklet of recipes first appeared in 1955 in response to requests for information and it has been reprinted several times. Due to enthusiastic endorsements of Cornell bread in the popular paperback *Feel Like A Million*, by Catharyn Elwood, and the health books of Ruth Adams and Frank Murray, as well as standard cookbooks such as *Fanny Farmer's* and Irma Rombauer's *The Joy of Cooking*, the demand for an improved bread has not only continued, but is growing. Magazine articles helped to spread the news. Hundreds of inquiries came from a letter printed in the *Ladies' Home Journal* in 1953. Jean Hewitt in the *New York Times Sunday Magazine* named Cornell bread "The Do-Good Loaf." The recipe was reprinted among the *Times'* most requested recipes for 1972.

The recipe for Cornell bread is now more in demand than ever. In response to the letters of inquiry and appreciation coming from school children, teachers, homemakers, business people and professionals, I have revised and expanded the previous booklet. Many new recipes have been added and some of the original ones have been modified slightly to make them easier and even more foolproof. I have included additional photographs which illustrate the step-by-step instructions in great detail.

Some of the mail comes from people who are old hands at baking, while others admit that this is their first venture. Clive would be delighted with their enthusiasm for better nutrition, especially that of the young families and the men who are doing their own home baking. As a boy, before his days at the University of Illinois and graduate studies at Berkeley, California, he would count the calories and vitamins at the family table. Later, and all during his life he enjoyed cooking and would often entertain visiting professors with an evening of baking bread. This edition, like the original publication, includes excerpts from his talks and writings about the bread and its special ingredients. These excerpts are printed in italics and with his initials.

I hope that you will join in the movement to achieve better bread in your home and in your community.

—JEANETTE B. McCAY

Englewood, Florida
February, 1980

What Makes It "Cornell"?

The special features of the Cornell bread that make it different from ordinary bread are the additions of *soy flour, nonfat dry milk* and *wheat germ.*

SOY FLOUR, made from soybeans, the most valuable cash crop in the United States, is a rich protein concentrate, with over 40 percent protein. Most important, it supplies the protein building blocks (called amino acids) that are lacking in wheat. The combination of soy and wheat makes the protein complete and compares favorably to the protein value of meat.

In addition to its protein, soy flour also supplies calcium, iron, phosphorus, and magnesium, as well as B vitamins and lecithin.

The full-fat soy flour is preferred to the defatted because of the better appearance and eating quality it gives the baked foods. Since the fatty acids of soy oil are unsaturated they do not add cholesterol to the blood.

Soy flour gives a warm golden color to the crumb, a rich flavor and good keeping quality. It is included in many commercial formulas for doughnuts, cakes and other baked goods. Full-fat soy is sometimes marketed as "whole grain" or "natural."

NONFAT DRY MILK, one of the bargain foods in America, has about twice the protein value of meat. Like soy, milk complements the incomplete protein blocks of wheat. Milk is also a good source of the mineral calcium, so important in the health and maintenance of bones and teeth. Its liberal amounts of riboflavin are essential for good eyesight.

WHEAT GERM, that part of the wheat kernel that contains the life force of the plant, is needed for growth with its protein, iron, vitamin E and B vitamins. It is a food whose value has been demonstrated by centuries of human experience.

The mixture of these three foods with wheat flour in bread so improves its quality that animals can live healthily on *only* this bread with butter. Repeated experiments at Cornell University, the University of Rochester, and other nutrition laboratories have demonstrated that animals such as the white rat can grow and reproduce even through succeeding generations when fed on only Cornell bread and butter. In contrast, their brothers and sisters fed ordinary breads do not grow normally. Their fur becomes thin, their tails and paws grow scaly and sore, and they waste away and die prematurely.

Though Cornell bread has only a little more protein than the usual white bread, it is the *quality* of the combined proteins that gives the power of growth. You may not plan to live on bread and butter alone, but it is good to know that Cornell bread can contribute to your health with its protein, its calcium and B vitamins—all needed by young and old alike.

When one realizes that it takes 16 pounds of grain and soy fed to an animal in order to produce 1 pound of beef, 6 pounds for 1 pound of pork, 4 pounds for 1 pound of turkey and 3 pounds of feed for 1 pound of chicken, one can feel virtuous when reducing the amount of animal protein on the table. When you are serving the high-protein Cornell bread, you are freeing more grain and soy for the hungry people of the world. Let the price of meat skyrocket at the butcher shop and rest content that your family's health will not suffer with less meat, if Cornell bread is on the table!

The use of Cornell bread need not upset your special diet, since the formula can be adjusted in nearly every respect.

SALT: If you are on a low-salt diet, the salt can be eliminated, or a substitute used. We have specified sea salt, so as to obtain the trace minerals.

SUGAR: It can also be reduced or eliminated, or a substitute, such as fructose, used. We have specified honey, molasses or brown sugar for their additional minerals.

CHOLESTEROL: Shortening can be eliminated, if desired. We have chosen salad oil because of its low cholesterol.

ROUGHAGE: It can be reduced by using all white flour, or increased by adding bran, whole wheat, rye and other whole grains, as well as dried fruits.

Why did Clive choose "white" bread to improve instead of whole grain? Of course he knew the value of whole grains, but he also knew how difficult it is for humans to change their eating habits. He recognized that one must start improvement where one is—and then go on from there.

Once you get in the habit of enriching your bread, you can make cakes, cookies, piecrust and other baked products from your favorite recipes that will contain a more complete protein, more minerals and vitamins if you put 1 tablespoon of soy flour, 1 tablespoon of nonfat dry milk and 1 teaspoon of wheat germ in the bottom of the cup when you measure each cup of flour.

. . . Open-formula bread and foods make it possible for the housewife to judge relative merits of products. A bread containing two or three percent milk or even none may taste nearly as good as a bread containing wheat germ, soy flour and 8 percent milk, but it has much less value.—C.M.M.

Tips for Good Luck

It is just as easy to make good bread as it is to make good cake—and lots more fun! That is because you are working with yeast that is alive, introducing variables and giving yourself a chance to exercise your judgment. Each time you bake is a new adventure and each time your judgment improves along with the bread.

In our experience, the most important steps in home baking are the handling of the yeast (adjusting the warmth and time for the dough to rise) and the flour (how much to use and how long to knead). The commercial baker controls these factors. We hope these remarks will help you to control them, too.

YEAST, since it is a mass of microscopic plants, needs a certain amount of warmth to grow. Too much heat will kill it. Blood temperature, or liquid which feels just warm to your wrist, will always be safe.

There are two ways of adding yeast to your dough. The traditional method is to sprinkle the dry yeast on the warm liquid and let it soften and grow a little, while you prepare the remaining ingredients. The temperature given for this liquid is 105° to 115° F.

The so-called rapid-mix method is to mix the dry yeast with the dry ingredients and then to use a higher temperature for the liquid.

I have followed both methods successfully, but I am writing these recipes using the traditional one—casting my yeast upon the warm water. May I say here that old hands at bread-making must forgive my giving so many details, remembering that some readers will be beginners in the art.

In any case, it is essential to have warm ingredients, warm utensils and a cozily warm kitchen in which to work. In winter, flour and utensils can be warmed in the oven. You can protect the dough from chilling while it rises by placing the container in a larger bowl of hot water, or putting it in a warm oven with a dish of hot water on the shelf below. Or turn the oven heat on, count 15 and turn it off, remembering that this warmth is only for rising at about 80° F., not for baking.

While the yeast is growing on the starch and sugar in the dough, it will form alcohol and bubbles of carbon dioxide gas which inflate the mass. With the right warmth, the dough expands rapidly. But if the temperature is cooler, it will rise more slowly, and more time will be needed. Suggested times are given with each recipe, but do not worry if it takes longer in your situation. Just wait! Be patient!

One of the tests for a dough that has risen long enough is to press a finger into it. If the mark remains and the dough has doubled in size, it has risen long enough.

FLOUR, on which the yeast acts, contains gluten. It is a protein, rubbery and elastic, which traps and holds the

Figure 1. In winter, if your kitchen temperature is too cool, set the bowl in another bowl of hot water (not above 130° F.)

Figure 2. The finger test.

bubbles of gas that make the loaf light and porous.

When the gluten is strong, flour absorbs considerable water and produces high, "bold" loaves. When the gluten is weak, more flour must be used and the volume of the loaves will not be as large. This gluten has to supply the "spring" for all the healthful ingredients called for in Cornell bread, because the soy, the wheat germ and the milk can't help in this respect.

Kneading develops the strength of the gluten, so the first mixing of the flour and yeast solution should be vigorous and thorough. Punching, slapping, stirring in the bowl by hand, or with an electric mixer, is important. (Be sure the motor of your mixer is strong enough not to burn out.) Then turn the dough onto the board, with more flour if needed, and knead at least 5 minutes. Watch the clock and give full time. You'll see that the baker's formula specifies 12 to 15 minutes in an electric mixer. After long, thorough mixing, the dough should be easy to handle, but don't be afraid to add more flour if you're getting stuck up! For those who have trouble with sticky fingers, you can dress up the bread board with a clean cloth of coarse canvas or linen. Put the leg of a child's white sock (with the foot cut off) on the rolling pin. Rub flour into the fiber of the material thoroughly and you can handle most any dough without adding excess flour. When your baking is finished, shake off excess flour, fold the cloth and put away in a plastic bag till next time.

These recipes call for unbleached flour, which can be purchased in any grocery store, and is very satisfactory. Bread flour can also be obtained and has a stronger gluten than the unbleached. Therefore, you may need less of the bread flour.

You'll love the warm, velvety feeling of dough in your hands and the fragrance that fills the house with your baking. You'll love the inviting brown crust and golden crumb of Cornell bread—a bread that stays fresh and freezes well. Best of all, you'll love the way your family demolishes the fresh loaves—precious applause to one who is working for their well-being.

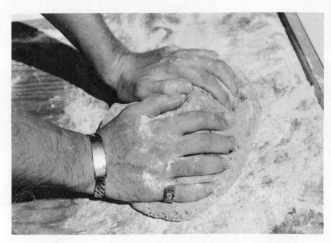

Figure 4. Give full time to kneading the dough.

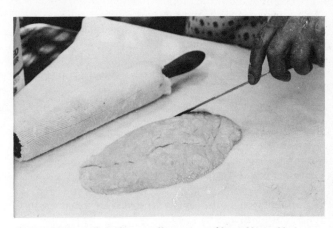

Figure 5. Floured cloths on rolling pin and bread board help prevent sticking.

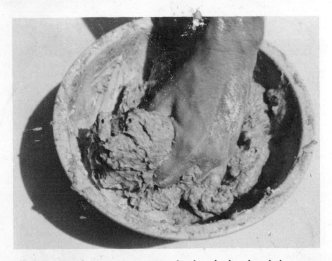

Figure 3. With vigorous mixing by hand, the dough becomes strong and elastic.

. . . In the past, magnesium has been given little attention in human nutrition, but it has become more important as research has shown that it will prevent and overcome the formation of stones in the bladder and the calcification of the soft tissues of the kidneys. Other studies indicate that it is helpful in treating high blood pressure and difficulties with the heart. A typical person excretes about a fifth of a gram of magnesium per day. To keep in balance, this must be replaced.—C.M.M.

. . . The ability of old rats to select diets adequate in calcium seems to decline as age advances. In early life the young rat has the ability to select a diet containing calcium. In middle life this ability declines . . . In old age the rat becomes an "old fool" and will die while drinking a 10% sugar solution to satisfy its taste rather than eating a diet to meet its nutritional requirements. Thus in old age when the body's need for calcium in the diet increases, the ability to select this diet seems to disappear. This may also apply to the human diet.—C.M.M.

. . . The deterioration of the skeleton in man and experimental animals has long been recognized as a characteristic of aging . . . . Modern evidence indicates that the deterioration of the skeleton reflects the quality of the diet, changes in the endocrines such as the parathyroids and other factors such as the amount of exercise . . . . There is substantial evidence that human diets adequate in calcium tend to maintain the quality of bone even under adverse action of the parathyroids.—C.M.M.

The Basic Cornell "White" Bread Recipe

[makes 3 loaves]

This recipe forms the foundation for the entire book. Once you have mastered this, you'll be anxious to try your hand at the many interesting and delicious variations. Also called "Golden Triple Rich " by the Ithaca Co-op Food Store, where it was first sold commercially in the 1950's. The bread is not actually white, but a pleasing creamy color.

PLACE in a large mixing bowl, and LET STAND:

    3 cups warm water (105° to 115° F.)
    2 packages or 2 tablespoons active dry yeast
    2 tablespoons honey or brown sugar
    3 teaspoons sea salt
    2 tablespoons salad oil

MEASURE and STIR together:

    6 cups unbleached flour
    3 tablespoons wheat germ
    ½ cup full-fat soy flour
    ¾ cup nonfat dry milk

STIR the liquids and ADD while stirring:

    ½ to ¾ the flour mixture

BEAT vigorously, about 75 strokes by hand, or 2 minutes with electric mixer.

ADD remainder of flour mixture.

WORK and MIX flour in thoroughly and vigorously by hand 5 minutes. At first the dough will be sticky as you grasp it. Beat it, turning it round and round in the bowl. At the end of this time you'll feel it change and become firmer.

TURN dough onto floured board and KNEAD using 1 to 3 cups more flour, as needed, to make the dough smooth.

PLACE in an oiled bowl. Grease top of dough lightly and cover.

LET RISE in a warm place until double in size, about 1 hour. (Fingerprint remains when dough has risen enough.) If the room is cold, place bowl in another bowl of hot water.

PUNCH dough down, fold over edges and turn upside down to rise another 20 minutes, or until double again.

TURN onto board, and divide dough into 3 portions. Fold each into the center to make smooth, tight balls. Cover and let stand 10 minutes on the board while you oil the baking pans.

SHAPE into 3 loaves or 2 loaves and a pan of rolls.

Figure 7. Punch dough down after first rising.

Figure 6. Add the flour ingredients gradually, beating with an electric mixer or egg beater as long as you can.

Figure 8. Dividing the dough into portions.

Figure 10. Bread has risen in pans and is ready to bake.

Figure 11. Bread has come from the oven and is removed from pan to cool.

Figure 9. Forming a loaf.

TO SHAPE A LOAF: Flatten ball on the board with hands into a rectangle. Then fold each long side to the center. Then roll this small rectangle to make a loaf. Press ends to seal. Turn seam down.

TO SHAPE ROLLS: Squeeze off bits of dough and shape like golf balls. These may be baked in muffin pans or all together in a cake pan.

PLACE shaped dough in oiled pans. Loaf pans should be about 8½ x 4½ x 2½ inches in size.

LET RISE in pans until double in size, about 45 minutes.

BAKE in a moderate oven, 350° F., for 50 to 60 minutes (about 30 minutes for rolls). If the loaves begin to brown in 15 or 20 minutes, reduce the temperature. Bread is done if it sounds hollow when tapped.

REMOVE bread from the pans and put on a rack or cloth to cool. Brush with oil if a thin, tender crust is desired. Let cool completely before wrapping and storing or freezing.

Since this bread contains no preservative as the commercial loaves usually do, keep it in the freezer. Reheat frozen bread a few minutes at 300° F. before serving.

The Cornell dough refrigerates beautifully. It can be stored in a covered container in the cold before it is formed. When ready to use, punch it down, shape it, place in baking pan, let rise to double in a warm place and bake as usual. Or shape it before it goes into the refrigerator, place in baking pan, grease the top of the dough and cover with plastic so it won't dry out. While it is stored in the cold, it will gradually rise. When ready to use, let it stand in a warm room 15 or 20 minutes, then bake as usual.

This is such a convenient way to have freshly baked bread on a busy day.

Figure 12. Some of the variations you can make from the basic "white" bread recipe—breadsticks, crusty French bread, cracked wheat and cornmeal breads.

VARIATIONS ON THE BASIC CORNELL RECIPE

First master the basic Cornell bread, for it is the grand-daddy of all the Cornell recipes that follow. Practice makes perfect, and you will be able to make dozens of varieties—all with the health values of improved protein.

Sprouted Grain Bread

For a wonderful flavor and chewy texture, perhaps my favorite variation of the basic Cornell recipe is to add sprouted wheat or rye. About the only adjustment you will need to make is in the amount of flour used.

Obtain clean kernels of wheat or rye. Cover 1 cup of whole kernels with warm water and let stand in a warm room overnight. In the morning, drain off the water and cover with fresh. Let stand in a warm place for another day and night. Drain several times and add fresh water.

By the end of the second day, the grain will have become much softer and more chewy. The one cupful will have swelled to two cups and small, white sprouts may begin to show.

From this time on, drain the kernels and keep them covered in the refrigerator until you are ready to make bread. Rinse the grain at intervals with fresh water so it will not dry out.

For your bread, put the sprouted grain through the food chopper, using the finest blade. You'll be interested to see

Figure 13. Whole grains, softened and sprouted by standing in warm water for several days, are put through a food mill for a delicious bread.

how sticky and elastic it is. Add the ground-up kernels with the flour in your Cornell recipe. It may require more or less flour than usual to give the right consistency for kneading. Add the remainder of the ingredients and proceed as usual.

Try this once and you'll repeat it. The loaf is moist and chewy like the wheat and some claim it is the most delicious bread they've ever eaten.

Herb Breads

For a new turn to the basic Cornell recipe and a treat to bring acclaim, add your favorite herbs to the formula along with the dry ingredients. Minnie Muenscher, in her

Herb Cookbook, suggests:

    3 teaspoons savory
    1 teaspoon marjoram
    1½ teaspoons parsley
    ½ teaspoon thyme

Or to be different, roll the dough into a sheet, sprinkle with the crushed herbs and shake on some Parmesan cheese. Roll up like a jelly roll. Put on greased tins and let rise and bake.

Herb breads are good with soups and salads, as sandwiches or toast. Yes, really good! A friend now demands some herbs in every baking his wife makes.

Bread Sticks

[a protein addition to the soup or salad course]

Whenever you have some spare dough, make it up into small balls. Roll each one into a long, thin stick. Place sticks on greased baking sheet. Let rise. Brush with egg white and water beaten together. Sprinkle with sesame or poppy seeds. Bake at 375° F. until lightly browned.

Fifty-fifty Whole Wheat Bread

For a delicious bread containing whole wheat's nutritional values, follow the Cornell recipe, using half whole wheat and half white flour. The bread will be light and tasty. For many families, this is their regular choice for baking week after week.

Of course, other combinations of flour, such as rye, millet, bran, oat, cornmeal, buckwheat, and a little ground flaxseed can also replace part of the white. One homemaker also adds 1 teaspoon of cinnamon and 1 cup of raisins to the mixture.

A home or bakery electric mill to grind your own grain into a fine flour can be bought. Many health-food stores have flour mills and will grind grain to order for you, saving you trouble and the problem of where to store a mill. You'll enjoy the flavor of freshly milled whole grain.

Figure 14. Loaves of fifty-fifty whole wheat bread fresh from the oven.

Figure 15. Hamburger buns have risen and are ready to bake.

Hamburger Buns

Don't forget hamburgers! When the Cornell dough is ready to bake, roll it out about an inch thick. Cut into rounds with a big cookie cutter. Brush over with a little egg white beaten with an equal amount of water. Sprinkle with sesame seeds. Let rise to double in size and bake in a 350° F. oven about 20 minutes, until done.

Pizza

[a true meal that only needs a salad
to make it completely satisfying]

MAKE up the basic Cornell dough, using some whole wheat or rye with the white flour if desired. After the second rising, when the dough is ready to shape, divide it into thirds.

FLATTEN each third to about ¼ inch thick onto an oiled pizza pan. Cover with a layer of hot country sausage that has been crumbled and lightly browned in a skillet.

COVER this with a seasoned tomato sauce (made of tomato paste thinned with water, herbs such as marjoram, thyme, rosemary, sage and oregano, or your own favorite).

SPRINKLE on crumbled mozzarella cheese, minced onion, green pepper.

COVER with slices of pepperoni sausage and a final treatment of Parmesan cheese.

LET RISE for 15 minutes.

BAKE 15 minutes at 425° F. and serve at once.

Pita, The Pocket Bread

Flat breads make fascinating fare in this day of snacks and finger foods, whether it's Mexican *tortilla*, Indian *chapati*, or Middle Eastern *pita*. They are similar in their ability to offer the covering for a filled sandwich that is tasty and different. And if they contain improved protein of the Cornell recipe and are filled with an extended meat mixture, you've a main dish for a picnic or patio supper that is satisfying, as well as interesting to family and guests.

Figure 16. Cornell pizza makes a snack or a meal that is tasty *and* nutritious.

Figure 17. When the *pitas* bake, they puff up and make pockets. Here two are cut open and all ready for a delicious filling, such as chicken or tuna salad.

MAKE up the basic "white" bread dough. After the second rising, SHAPE dough into balls about the size of lemons. Roll in cornmeal.

FLATTEN these into rounds about ¼ inch thick. Place on an oiled baking sheet.

LET RISE for 20 to 30 minutes and BAKE at 425° F. about 10 minutes, until golden brown.

Whole Wheat and Carrot Pita

[makes about 12 pitas]

Here is another interesting recipe for *pita*, made with whole wheat and carrots—delicious and easy if you have a blender or food processor. This recipe can also be used for Mexican *tortillas*.

PLACE in mixing bowl and let dissolve:
  2½ cups warm water (105° to 115° F.)
  1 package active dry yeast
Meanwhile PREPARE:
  2 cups finely grated carrots
  3 teaspoons sea salt
ADD carrots and salt to yeast mixture and STIR IN to make a soft dough:
  3 tablespoons wheat germ
  ½ cup full-fat soy flour
  ¾ cup nonfat dry milk
  4 to 5 cups whole wheat flour
TURN onto board and ADD more flour until dough can be handled.
KNEAD 5 to 10 minutes, until smooth.
FOR PITAS:
PULL off a ball of dough the size of a lemon.
PRESS ball of dough into cornmeal on all sides.
ROLL out into a circle ¼ thick.
PLACE ON an oiled pan, and let rest about 20 to 30 minutes.
BAKE at 425° F. until brown and puffy, about 10 minutes.
FOR TORTILLAS:
PULL off a piece of dough the size of a golf ball.
ROLL out on a board covered with cornmeal into very, very thin circles.
PLACE each on a hot heavy skillet, without oil and cook a few minutes on each side, until light brown. Tortillas should be soft.

French-Style Bread

[also for Cuban, Italian and Viennese styles]

While you are working with the basic "white" recipe, you must manipulate it *à la française* for a change. If there is any bread that has earned paeans of praise—"crusty, crisp outside, loose and open inside, hearty, satisfying, flavorful, downright delicious, etc. etc.," it is the common bread of France. Italian, Cuban and Viennese breads are also favorites in the same crusty style.

These are all water breads, baked on the floor of the oven at high temperature with steam. While the Cornell formula will not duplicate the French, it can also be crisp and crusty and far more valuable healthwise.

Here's how:

MAKE up the Cornell "white" bread dough. Follow directions for mixing. Let the dough be soft. Mix it thoroughly in the bowl, then turn it onto the board to knead with a little more flour. Let rise in the greased bowl to double its size, at a cooler temperature if possible, 70° to 78° F., for 1 to 1½ hours.

TURN onto floured board, adding a little more flour if necessary. Round up. Cover and let rise on board to double again. Divide into four balls.

LET RISE while you oil 2 baking sheets.

SHAPE the balls into loaves which may be long and narrow, 15 x 2 inches, or round.

PLACE on the baking sheets. LET RISE to double in size. With a sharp knife or razor, cut diagonal slashes in the top of the long loaves and a cross on the round ones. A

Figure 18. For a Continental touch, try the French-style Cornell loaf.

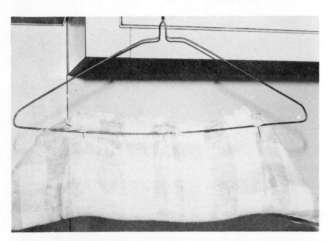

Figure 19. Instead of investing in a French bread pan to give round loaves, I hung the loaf from a floured cloth to prevent it from flattening.

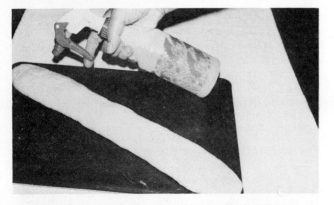

Figure 20. Spraying the loaves with water helps to keep the crust crisp and thin.

sprinkling of sesame seeds is delicious, but first brush on egg white mixed with a little water to make them stick.

INDUCE steam by spraying the loaves with water, and place a shallow pan of boiling water in the bottom of a hot oven, 425° F. One Francophile puts a few ice cubes in the oven. The idea is to have steam for the first few minutes of baking so the dough will expand fully without making a heavy crust.

BAKE the loaves at 425° F. about 30 minutes in all, or until they brown and sound hollow when tapped. Cool on a rack.

When freshly baked, this bread is delightfully crusty. Wrap it carefully and store in the freezer. Heat before serving to restore the crispness.

Crusty Rolls

When you are making up the Cornell dough, save part of it for hard, crusty rolls. After the second rising, form the dough into 16 or 18 balls. Place on an oiled baking sheet. Cover. Let rise till double, about 45 minutes. Brush with egg white and water and sprinkle with sesame or poppy seeds. Spray with water. Bake at 425° F., as for the French bread above, with a shallow pan of boiling water in the bottom of the oven. They should be done in 10 to 12 minutes.

. . . Even in his choice of sweet substances one can choose honey or dark molasses such as the sorghums that provide other foodstuffs than mere sugar. Many of these substances are little understood today but we know they exist.— C.M.M.

Figure 21. The finger test tells when rolls, as well as loaves, have risen long enough.

Figure 22. Crusty rolls cool on a rack.

Figure 23. Forming the potato rolls.

Figure 24. Rolls have risen and are ready to bake.

Refrigerator Potato Rolls

[makes 3 to 4 dozen rolls]

BOIL 3 medium-sized potatoes until soft, saving the potato water. MASH. (Or make up 1 cup of instant mashed potatoes according to directions on package.) COOL.

PLACE in a large bowl, and LET STAND for 5 minutes:
 1 cup warm water (105° to 115° F.). Part may be potato water
 2 packages active dry yeast

ADD:
 ½ cup salad oil
 ⅓ cup honey, brown sugar or fructose
 2 teaspoons sea salt
 1 cup mashed potatoes, cooled
 2 eggs (reserve a little egg white to brush tops of rolls)
 3 tablespoons wheat germ
 ⅓ cup full-fat soy flour
 ½ cup nonfat dry milk

STIR and gradually ADD:
 5 to 6 cups unbleached flour (you may substitute 1 or 2 cups of whole wheat, bran or rye for part of the white flour)

. . . The decline in the use of potatoes is another tragedy in the American nutrition picture. Every study of potatoes made in our laboratory creates renewed respect for this superb food—one of the best ever discovered by man. But people who suffer from lack of exercise prefer not to work their flabby muscles in carrying a bag of potatoes up the apartment stairs.—C.M.M.

. . . Potatoes seem to favor a long span of life.—C.M.M.

. . . Potatoes are excellent food for all ages. The best supplement for them is milk or cheese. In tests with potatoes using laboratory animals such as white rats, it has been found that this food is one of the best to insure long life with good health. Even bread is a good supplement for potatoes.—C.M.M.

BEAT for as long as possible with egg beater or electric mixer.

TURN dough out on a floured board or cloth, using more flour as needed, but keeping dough soft. KNEAD lightly.

PLACE in oiled bowl. Grease top of dough. Cover container and set in refrigerator until needed. (If desired, the rolls can be shaped, allowed to rise, and baked without refrigerating. Or divide the dough—use half immediately and chill the rest for a later day.)

REMOVE dough from refrigerator and shape into pocketbook rolls.

FLATTEN dough with a rolling pin. CUT OUT rounds, brushing each with melted butter. FOLD OVER and place on oiled baking pan. PAINT rolls with egg white stirred with a little water. SPRINKLE with sesame seed.

LET RISE to double in size. If the dough is cold it will take longer, but if it has not been chilled, 20 minutes may be enough time.

BAKE at 350° F. for about 20 minutes.

STORE in plastic bags in deep freeze, and reheat before serving.

. . . Dry nutritional yeast is a unique food that is coming into modern use. In olden times men drank yeast suspended in beer and the bakery was often located near the brewery since the baker drew his supply of live yeast from the brewery. In modern times much yeast is dried after it is removed from making beer. A pound of dry yeast is produced from every hundred gallons of beer. Yeast is very rich in all water-soluble vitamins except B12. It contains about twice as much protein as meat and its protein is a very good supplement for wheat protein. Thus bread containing six per cent of nutritional yeast has high protein value.—C.M.M.

. . . Some time ago a writer described "enrichment" in regard to wheat flour as analogous to saying that a thief enriched one if he first stole all the silverware from a household and then returned a few spoons.—C.M.M.

. . . Even a vegetarian diet provides adequate iron if it contains liberal amounts of vegetables, whole wheat bread, and dark molasses. Whole wheat bread contains the wheat germ, which is a remarkable storehouse for many inorganic essentials such as iron and manganese.—C.M.M.

Cornell Pot and Batter Breads

Many busy homemakers enjoy making "easy-mix" and "no-knead" loaves and rolls. The basic "white" and other Cornell bread recipes can be used in this way.

Beat all ingredients well, as they are added, until a soft dough is formed. Remove all particles of dough from the sides of the bowl. Brush the surface with oil. Cover and let rise in a warm place until double.

You can either punch the dough down and let it rise a second time, or stir it briskly a few seconds and pour it into oiled pans or a casserole. Let rise and bake as usual.

This bread will not compete with your standard loaves. But when served warm in a casserole or pot, it makes a delicious luncheon or breakfast bread.

The batter breads make a good introduction for the first-time baker who is frightened at the thought of kneading dough, letting it rise, and using all that "judgment." My guess is that after a few batter breads and some sticky fingers, you'll be punching and kneading with the best of them!

Yeast-Raised Corn Bread

[makes 2 round loaves that
are delicious for breakfast or supper]

PLACE in mixing bowl:
  1½ cups warm water (105° to 115° F.)
  2 packages active dry yeast
  ⅓ cup honey or brown sugar

  2 teaspoons sea salt
  ½ cup salad oil
  2 eggs (room temperature)
STIR and BEAT IN gradually:
  1½ tablespoons wheat germ
  ¼ cup full-fat soy flour
  ⅓ cup nonfat dry milk
  1½ cups yellow cornmeal
  3½ cups unbleached flour
BEAT until well blended. Batter will be somewhat stiff.
DIVIDE batter between two oiled 8-inch round cake pans
  or cast-iron skillets.
COVER and LET RISE in a warm place until doubled,
  about 1 hour.
BAKE at 375° F. for 30 minutes, or until done. Serve
  warm.

A cup of crumbled cooked sausage or bacon may be added to the batter.

100% Whole Wheat Batter Bread

[makes 3 loaves or 2 loaves and a pan of muffins]

PLACE in mixing bowl:
  3 cups warm water (105° to 115° F.)
  2 packages active dry yeast
  2 tablespoons honey or molasses
  2 tablespoons salad oil
  3 teaspoons sea salt

Figure 25. Fresh batter bread makes any luncheon a special occasion, with very little work.

1 egg (room temperature)
LET STAND while you measure out:
3 tablespoons wheat germ
½ cup full-fat soy flour
¾ cup nonfat dry milk
5 cups whole wheat flour
1 cup raisins (if desired)
BLEND all the ingredients together thoroughly, using
your egg beater or mixer as long as you can, then continue mixing and beating with your hand. This makes a
sticky, loose dough and you may need more flour to
make it shape up.
PAT dough down to the bottom and clean sides of bowl.
Oil the top of the dough and sides of bowl. Cover.
LET RISE in a warm place until almost double in size,
about 30 to 40 minutes.
TURN onto board and SHAPE into 3 loaves 8½ x 4½ x
2½ or 2 loaves and 12 muffins. Use spatula to help handle this soft dough.
PLACE in oiled bread pans or muffin tins.
LET RISE until dough doubles.
BAKE at 400° F. for 15 minutes. Reduce temperature to
350° F. for 45 minutes, until loaves are brown and sound
hollow when tapped.
COOL on a rack. Wrap in plastic and store in freezer.

Figure 26. Spoon batter into greased and floured muffin tin.

No-Knead Dilly Rolls

PLACE in a large mixing bowl:
1 cup warm water (105° to 115° F.)
1 package active dry yeast
2 tablespoons honey or brown sugar
4 tablespoons salad oil
1 teaspoon sea salt
1 cup small-curd cottage cheese
3 teaspoons dill weed
¼ cup minced onion (if desired)
½ cup bran
1 egg
STIR all together, then BLEND IN:
1½ tablespoons wheat germ
¼ cup full-fat soy flour
⅓ cup nonfat dry milk
3½ to 4 cups unbleached flour
BEAT all ingredients together well. Dough will be sticky.
COVER bowl and LET STAND 25 minutes.
SPOON dough into 18 oiled and floured muffin cups or 6
cups and a casserole.
COVER and LET RISE in a warm place about 30 to 40
minutes.
BAKE in preheated oven at 350° F. for about 25 minutes.
They will be light brown. A casserole or a bread pan, 9 x
5 x 3 inches, will need 30 to 40 minutes to bake.

Figure 27. Sally Lunn cake ready to bake.

*. . . My interest in bread arose when I came to appreciate
the important part this primary foodstuff plays in the food
pattern of older people. This importance is due to many
factors such as low income, dependence upon prepared
foods, poor dentures, and genuine need during the declin-
ing years for a strong "staff of life."—C.M.M.*

Figure 28. Holiday fruit breads are welcome accompaniments
to tea or coffee any time of the year.

Sally Lunn

[makes 1 large loaf]

A famous sweet batter bread is Sally Lunn, which is said to be a corruption of the French *soleil lune*, or sun and moon cake. With our additions of spice, brown sugar, citron or dried fruits, it isn't so yellow and white as the original must have been when made with butter and white sugar. But do make up a fresh Sally Lunn for special tea or coffee guests.

PLACE in mixing bowl:
    1 cup warm water (105° to 115° F.)
    1 package active dry yeast
LET STAND while you measure and ADD:
    ⅓ cup honey, brown sugar or fructose
    1 teaspoon sea salt
    ½ cup salad oil
    3 eggs at room temperature
    1½ tablespoons wheat germ
    ¼ cup full-fat soy flour
    ⅓ cup nonfat dry milk
    ½ teaspoon cinnamon
    ¼ teaspoon nutmeg
    3½ cups unbleached flour
BEAT mixture for 3 minutes, using a spoon or electric mixer.
ADD ½ cup of any dried fruit, such as citron, raisins, cherries, or chopped apricots, and ½ cup of broken nuts, if desired.
BEAT in more flour, if needed, to make a stiff batter.
COVER the bowl and let rise in a warm place to double in size, about 1 hour.
STIR batter and pour into oiled and floured angel food pan.
COVER and LET RISE again for almost an hour until double in size.
SPRINKLE over the top a mixture of 3 tablespoons sugar, ½ teaspoon cinnamon and ¼ teaspoon nutmeg.
BAKE for 40 to 50 minutes in moderate oven, 350° F., until done.
REMOVE carefully from the pan, as this cake is large and fragile. Serve warm.

Raised Fruitcake

More fruits and nuts may be added to the batter for a holiday coffee cake such as this.
MAKE the Cornell Sally Lunn batter and ADD to it:
    1 cup soft prunes, chopped
    1 cup dates, pitted and chopped
    ½ cup soft apricots, chopped
    ½ cup raisins
    ½ cup each walnuts and almonds, chopped
    1 cup candied fruit
    8 cardamon seeds, shelled and crushed
Continue and bake as for the Sally Lunn.

Czech Babovka

[Czechoslovakian Easter bread]

MAKE the Sally Lunn batter and to it ADD:
    ½ teaspoon almond extract
    1 cup golden raisins
    ½ cup almonds, finely chopped
    6 candied cherries, sliced
    1 tablespoon grated orange rind
After the first rising, stir in fruit and nuts. Pour into an oiled and floured crown mold or angel cake pan and proceed as for Sally Lunn cake.

. . . Some plant foods such as sesame contain substantial amounts of calcium. Sesame seeds are staple articles of diet in many areas. Such seeds should be eaten without the removal of the husks because these contain the calcium.
—C.M.M.

. . . In tests with white rats, eggs were fed as ten per cent of the dry diet for the whole of life. No special diseases were observed in old age and the life span of the animals was normal. Hence from such animal tests there is no evidence that eggs are injurious. Since the egg serves as a complete food it may insure the older person in regard to protein and vitamins as well as iron and trace minerals.
—C.M.M.

Cornell Health Breads

It's a puzzlement—to call some "health" foods, when all food should be healthful. But we do have to admit there are "junk" foods that yield only "naughty" calories as a doctor friend calls them—the white flour, white sugar, white fat mixtures that are detrimental to the obese, the diabetic, the heart patient and others whose health is threatened.

So we go to the "natural food" stores, grateful to find a splendid array of high-quality nutritional ingredients. Fortunately, regular groceries are catching on and now offer a greater variety of whole grains, dark molasses, honey, seeds, sprouted beans, nuts and dried fruits.

Many of the breads baked by young people for their community meals and markets combine an imaginative mixture of these natural foods. A letter from a young friend says, "I have just discovered the natural foods 'trip' and I find it really satisfying that I am giving myself the best food."

When making the dark breads, I usually use half-size tins, because the special loaves make such popular gifts. Also it is easier to cut the heavier bread in thinner slices.

Figure 29. When rye bread is almost done, brush it with milk, salt water or cornstarch solution for a tough, shiny crust.

Rye Bread with Beer

[makes 2 loaves]

PLACE in mixing bowl:
  1 12-oz. can (1½ cups) warm beer (105° to 115° F.)
  1 package active dry yeast
  ½ cup dark molasses (if desired)
  2 tablespoons salad oil
  2 teaspoons sea salt
  1 tablespoon caraway seeds, crushed
MEASURE and MIX together in another bowl:
  2 tablespoons wheat germ
  ¼ cup full-fat soy flour
  ⅓ cup nonfat dry milk
  1½ cups rye flour
  1½ cups unbleached flour
STIR the liquids and ADD while stirring:
  The flour mixture
BEAT vigorously, about 75 strokes by hand, or 2 minutes with electric mixer.
ADD more flour, if needed, to make a soft dough.
BEAT thoroughly and vigorously.
TURN dough onto floured board, using more of the rye and white flour as needed.
KNEAD 5 minutes to make the dough smooth.
PLACE in an oiled bowl. Cover with plastic.
LET RISE in a warm place until double in size, about an hour.

PUNCH dough down, fold edges under, turn upside down to rise to double again.
TURN onto board, and divide into 2 portions.
FOLD each into the center to make 2 smooth, tight balls for round loaves, or stretch out into 2 long loaves.
PLACE on a greased baking sheet.
LET RISE until double in size, about 1 hour. With a sharp knife or razor, make several slashes across the tops.
BAKE in a moderate oven, 350° F., for 30 to 40 minutes, until loaves sound hollow when tapped.
REMOVE from pan and cool on a rack.

If you do not wish to use beer, you can substitute warm water, warm potato water, or warm buttermilk. Cornmeal is often sprinkled over the baking sheet to give a crisp bottom crust. Also, sometimes the loaves are brushed with milk, salt water (½ teaspoon salt in ¼ cup water), or a teaspoon of cornstarch dissolved in ¼ cup cold water, during the last few minutes of baking to give a tough, shiny crust.

Swedish Limpa Bread

To give that characteristic flavor, make up the Cornell rye bread, with the beer. In addition to the caraway seeds (or without them), add ½ teaspoon ground anise seed, and 2 teaspoons of grated orange rind. Proceed as for the Cornell rye.

. . . For three centuries the people of Ireland, Poland, Wales, and many other parts of the world have derived both energy and protein from the potato.—C.M.M.

John's Oatmeal Porridge Bread

[makes 3 loaves]

MIX together in large bowl:
  3 cups boiling water
  2 cups oatmeal, uncooked (or other whole grain breakfast cereal, such as wheat or a mixture of grains)
LET COOL to 105° to 115° F. and ADD:
  2 packages active dry yeast
STIR to soften yeast and ADD:
  3 tablespoons salad oil
  ⅓ cup honey, brown sugar or molasses
  3 teaspoons sea salt
  ¼ cup sesame seeds
  1 cup raisins, dates or prunes
MEASURE and STIR IN:
  3 tablespoons wheat germ
  ½ cup full-fat soy flour
  ¾ cup nonfat dry milk
  1 cup rye, buckwheat or whole wheat flour
STIR IN:
  2 to 3 cups unbleached flour
BEAT about 75 strokes by hand, or 2 minutes with the
  electric mixer.
MIX IN more flour, if needed.
KNEAD until dough is smooth and elastic on board, about
  5 minutes.
PLACE dough in oiled bowl. Grease top lightly and cover.
LET RISE until nearly double in size, about an hour.
PUNCH DOWN, fold over edges and turn upside down to
  rise another 20 minutes.
TURN onto board and DIVIDE into 3 parts.
MAKE into smooth, tight balls. Cover and let stand 10
  minutes.
SHAPE into 3 loaves as described for white bread. Place
  in oiled tins. Oil tops lightly and cover. LET RISE until
  double in size, about 1 hour.

Figure 30. John's bread has risen and is ready to bake.

BAKE in moderate oven, 350° F., for about 60 minutes. If
  the loaves begin to brown in 15 or 20 minutes, reduce
  temperature to 325° F.
REMOVE the bread from the pans and put on a rack to
  cool.

Whole Wheat and Brewer's Yeast Bread

[makes 2 loaves]

PLACE in large bowl and STIR:
  2 cups warm water (105° to 115° F.)
  2 packages active dry yeast
  ¼ cup brown sugar
  ¼ cup dark molasses
  2 teaspoons sea salt
  2 tablespoons salad oil
  1 egg (room temperature)
MEASURE and STIR IN:
  1½ tablespoons wheat germ
  ¼ cup full-fat soy flour
  ⅓ cup nonfat dry milk
  2 tablespoons brewer's yeast
  2 tablespoons sesame seeds
  3 tablespoons Mexican pumpkin seeds, sunflower
    seeds or nuts
  ¼ cup raisins
  4½ cups whole wheat flour
BEAT as long as you can with an egg beater or electric
  mixer. Then continue mixing and beating with your
  hand for at least 5 minutes, until the dough becomes
  firm and elastic.
TURN onto floured board, using more flour if needed.
KNEAD and SHAPE into smooth ball. PLACE dough into
  oiled bowl.
LET RISE in warm place until double in size, about 1
  hour.
PUNCH DOWN, turn upside down and let rise another
  20 minutes.
DIVIDE dough into 2 portions. ROUND UP and let rest
  10 minutes while you oil 2 loaf pans.
SHAPE into 2 loaves as for white bread.
LET RISE for about an hour.
BAKE at 350° F. for about an hour, or until loaves
  sound hollow when tapped.
BRUSH tops with oil. Remove from pan and cool on
  rack.

BREWER'S YEAST, included with the dry ingredients,
is called "brewer's yeast" because it was a byproduct from
the brewing of beer. Now it is grown just for its nutritional
value. It is the foremost natural source of the B vitamins as
well as high-quality protein. Clive felt it was so valuable
that it should be used frequently. He encouraged our Co-op
Food Store to sell it by the pound, and homemakers to add
it to their baked foods. The flavor varies, according to the
brand, so experiment. You can increase the amount if you
desire.

*. . . The constant study of foods affords a pleasant hobby
since it can be followed in all parts of the world and in
much of the recorded history of man.—C.M.M.*

Cornell Sweet Doughs

Sweet yeast breads are favorites the world over. It would be fun to collect the stories and customs that center around these special coffee breads that appear at Christmas and Easter.

Fortunately, the recipes all adapt readily to the Cornell ingredients, which not only make them a little richer looking and tasting, but contribute their special nutrients and improve keeping quality as well.

Sticky Rolls

[makes 2 dozen rolls and 1 coffee ring]

Here we give the procedure for Cornell sticky rolls and indicate how it may be changed for some of the popular variants:

PLACE in large bowl, and LET STAND:
  2 cups warm water (105° to 115° F.)
  2 packages active dry yeast
  ½ cup honey, brown sugar or fructose
  ½ cup salad oil
  2 teaspoons sea salt
  2 eggs (room temperature)
MEASURE and STIR together:
  2 tablespoons wheat germ
  ⅓ cup full-fat soy flour
  ½ cup nonfat dry milk
  6 cups unbleached flour
STIR the yeast mixture and ADD while stirring:
  ½ to ¾ the flour mixture
BEAT vigorously, about 75 strokes by hand, or 2 minutes with electric mixer.
ADD remainder of flour mixture and beat it in thoroughly.
TURN OUT on a floured board, using 1 to 2 cups more flour if needed, but keeping dough soft.
KNEAD lightly and PLACE in an oiled bowl to rise. Grease top of dough lightly.
COVER and LET RISE in a warm place until double in size, about 1 hour.
PUNCH dough down, fold over edges and turn upside down to rise another 20 minutes.
TURN onto board and divide into two portions.
FOLD each in toward the center to make smooth, tight balls. Cover and let stand 10 minutes on the board.
GREASE 2 tins about 9 x 9 inches with butter or margarine. For a sticky surface, cover the bottom of the tin with a thin layer of brown sugar. Nuts can be added, if desired. Sprinkle with 2 tablespoons water.
ROLL dough to ¼ inch in thickness with rolling pin. Brush with melted butter, sprinkle with cinnamon, brown sugar, raisins, and broken nuts. Roll up like jelly roll.
FOR CINNAMON ROLLS: Slice and place cut sides

Figure 31. Dough rolled out for coffee cake and cinnamon rolls.

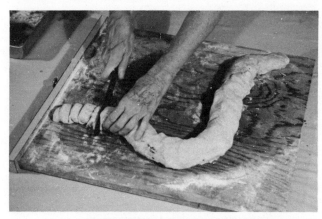

Figure 32. Slicing the dough for cinnamon rolls.

down on sugared tin to rise.

FOR COFFEE RING: Place roll on greased tin and join ends to form a ring. Pinch together. Cut top with scissors at one-inch intervals to show filling.
COVER and LET RISE in warm place until double in size, about 45 minutes.
BAKE in moderate oven, 350° F., for about 30 minutes. If rolls brown too fast, reduce the temperature or cover with foil.
REMOVE the sweet breads from the pans onto a rack to cool. Turn sticky rolls upside down.

Some other delicious fillings to roll up in the dough are:

APRICOT OR PRUNE: Cook dried fruits until soft, and sweeten to taste. Crush and cool. Add slivered almonds, if desired.

ORANGE: Warm together ¼ cup butter, ½ cup honey, grated rind of 1 large orange and 2 tablespoons orange juice. Cool.

Figure 33. Snipping the top of the coffee cake.

Figure 34. The sticky rolls, hot from the oven, are ready to be cooled on a rack.

HONEY, NUTS AND RAISINS: Warm together ⅓ cup honey, 1 cup nuts (sunflower seeds or pumpkin seeds), ½ cup butter, 2 teaspoons cinnamon, and 1 cup raisins. Cool and spread over dough.

ALMONDS AND FRUIT: ½ cup slivered almonds, grated rind and juice of 1 lemon, ½ cup candied citron and cherries, sprinkling of mace, and ½ cup raisins. Sprinkle over dough and roll up.

. . . Whole grain, dark flours should be the ones of choice unless people cannot tolerate their fiber. However such flours are subject to insect infestations because insects need many of the same vitamins as man. These flours also tend to become rancid and need to be stored in a cool place or even kept in a frozen food case. The old rule applies in the case of whole grain flours namely "select foods that perish readily, but eat them before they do!"—C.M.M.

Apple Coffee Cake

Press dough into greased round tin. Brush top with butter and press slices of cooking apple into it. Sprinkle with cinnamon and brown sugar. Let rise and bake.

German Christmas Stollen

Make up the Cornell dough for sticky rolls. When ready to shape knead in:
  1 cup raisins
  1 cup candied fruits
  1½ cups nuts, broken
  1 tablespoon cardamon seeds (remove seeds from their shells and crush in a mortar)
Divide dough into three balls. Let stand 10 minutes. Then press each ball into a flat oval. Fold the long way and press together firmly into a crescent. Put onto oiled baking sheet. Let rise and bake as usual. When cool, ice and decorate with more fruit and nuts, if desired.

Russian Kulitch

For *kulitch*, a Russian Easter cake, bake the stollen dough in large, deep tin cans, such as coffee comes in. Generously oil the cans and fill ½ to ⅔ full. Let rise till dough fills the cans and bake at 400° F. for 15 minutes. Reduce the temperature to 350° F., and continue baking for about 30 minutes more, until done. Remove from cans to cool. Ice and decorate as desired. Serve in slices about an inch thick. Return the top slice to the cake to keep it moist.

Italian Panettone

Panettone from Italy is another sweet bread, chock-full of candied fruits, raisins, and pine nuts, flavored with anise and baked in a high, round loaf. Again you can use the Cornell stollen recipe, adding the pignolias and anise. Before baking, cut a cross in the top with a sharp knife. This loaf can be decorated for serving.

Swedish Cardamon Braid

[makes 3 loaves]

Make up the sweet dough for Cornell sticky rolls. Add 8 cardamon seeds that have been freed from the shell and crushed. Some dried fruits may also be included, if desired.

Put the dough in an oiled bowl and let rise in a warm place until double in size. Punch down and let rise again. Divide into 3 balls. Divide each ball into 3 sections. Roll each section into a long, slender strand and make into 3 braids.

These may be put on an oiled baking sheet to rise, or in loaf tins. Either way, they look interesting.

When double in size, bake in a moderate oven, 350° F., about 30 minutes, or until they sound hollow when tapped. Cool on a rack and ice, if desired.

Figure 35. The cardamon braids are rising on an oiled baking sheet.

Figure 36. A good catch today—a Swedish cardamon braid.

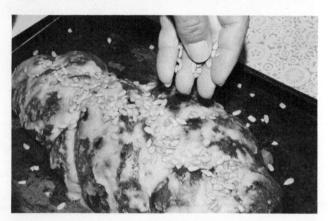

Figure 37. A sprinkling of sunflower seeds goes on top of the honey icing.

Brown Butter and Honey Glaze

Here is my favorite topping for sweet breads:
HEAT in a saucepan until lightly browned:
  2 tablespoons butter or margarine
ADD:
  4 tablespoons honey
  2 tablespoons lemon or orange juice with some grated rind (if desired)
STIR and COOL. THICKEN with:
  6 to 8 tablespoons powdered sugar
POUR on stollen or holiday cakes and sprinkle with sunflower seeds, nuts and dried fruits, as desired.

Figure 38. Shaping the butter horns.

Figure 39. Butter horns are always a hit and so much fun to make.

Butter Horn Rolls

Make up the Cornell sweet dough for sticky rolls. Let rise in bowl. After it has doubled in size, turn onto board. Divide into 2 or 3 portions. Roll each into a large pie shape about ¼ inch thick with a rolling pin. Spread with soft butter or margarine.

With a sharp knife or pastry wheel, cut into pie-shaped wedges. Roll up each one, starting at the widest side of the triangle. Curve a little to make a crescent. Put on oiled pan and let rise until light and double in size.

Brush each roll with a little egg white mixed with water. Sprinkle with sesame or poppy seeds.

Bake at 350° F. for about 10 minutes.

. . . Bread can be given increased nutritive value at an additional cost of about one cent per pound for the extra ingredients.—C.M.M.

. . . All that any of us can do is to make the best use of available knowledge. We all appreciate that this is seldom done.—C.M.M.

. . . For the preservation of strong bones, we have come to believe that milk in the latter half of life is fully as important for older people as milk in the first part of life.—C.M.M.

FOR FRENCH CROISSANTS: Chill the dough after the first rising. Roll it out thin. Cut cold butter or margarine into thin slivers and place over the dough. Fold the dough up and roll out again. Repeat several times, and then proceed as for the butter horns.

If you enjoyed making mud pies as a child, you'll love playing with dough, for it is delightfully malleable and you can feel its life in your fingers.

When the dough is ready to shape, instead of making it all into loaves, save out a portion for some creations. If you haven't time at the moment, put the dough in the refrigerator to use later.

There are the Parkerhouse or pocketbook rolls we used for the Cornell refrigerator potato rolls, described on page 11, and the butter horns on page 20.

Here are other suggestions:

CLOVER LEAF ROLLS: Shape dough into small balls, dip into melted butter, and put 3 little balls into each muffin cup.

LUCKY CLOVER: Put one larger ball into a muffin cup and then, with scissors, cut a cross in the top to divide the roll into fours.

DOUBLE DECKERS: Put one larger ball into a muffin cup. Brush the top with butter, and put a little ball of dough on top. If your dough is sweet, you will have a French brioche.

SNAILS: Form pieces of dough into slender ropes, about 6 inches long. Then coil each piece into a snail.

BOWKNOTS: Roll dough about ¼ inch thick. Brush with oil or butter. Cut in strips about ½ inch wide and 6 inches long. Tie in knots.

TWISTS: Roll the dough as for the knots, 8 inches long. Twist each end in opposite direction. Bring ends together and twist loop end.

Loaves, too, can carry your own trade mark. They can be cut with scissors to make a V-shaped design on top. They can be slashed with a sharp razor or knife to make long lines, or squares, or tic-tac-toe marks. Then how about dimples, just by pressing in a finger here and there?

Do all of this branding when the dough has already risen and is ready to bake.

Whole Wheat Yeast Doughnuts

[makes 3 dozen doughnuts with holes to match]

It may be a moot question in your family as to whether doughnuts are good for you. This is a decision we must each make for ourselves. However, there are millions of Americans who choose doughnuts daily as their favorite breakfast food.

If you are one of these, by all means make them contribute more than "naughty calories" by including the Cornell protein-improving ingredients of soy, milk and wheat germ. Fry them in cholesterol-free salad oil, such as corn or safflower oil. Use whole wheat, nutritional yeast, sesame seeds, honey, and sea salt to produce a food that will stick to the ribs and also add health values.

Clive was extremely practical and he believed that the popular, palatable doughnut could give a real slug of nutrition to the harried commuter's snack breakfast. He loved to make them himself.

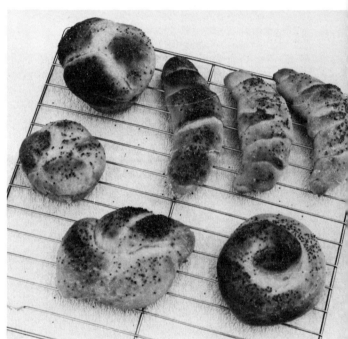

Figure 40. An array of Cornell rolls—before and after baking.

PLACE in a large bowl:
  1 cup warm water (105° to 115° F.)
  2 packages active dry yeast
  ¾ to 1 cup honey, brown sugar or fructose
  1 teaspoon sea salt
  ½ cup salad oil
  2 to 3 beaten eggs
LET STAND while you MEASURE and MIX together:
  2 cups unbleached flour
  2 cups whole wheat flour
  ¼ cup full-fat soy flour
  ⅓ cup nonfat dry milk
  ½ teaspoon cinnamon

Figure 41. Deep-frying doughnuts.

Figure 42. Doughnuts can be given a final dusting of powdered sugar.

¼ teaspoon nutmeg

2 tablespoons brewer's yeast (if desired)

2 tablespoons sesame seeds (if desired)

ADD flour mix gradually to the liquids, beating vigorously with an egg beater or electric mixer as long as you can.

ADD remainder of the mix, using your hand as beater. The dough will be soft.

PLACE dough in a greased bowl. Grease top. Cover with plastic. Refrigerate overnight.

PLACE desired amount on floured board. ROLL to 1 inch thick. CUT OUT with doughnut cutter. LET RISE 30 minutes and FRY in deep oil, heated to 360° to 370° F. Brown on each side and drain on paper towels.

SPRINKLE with sugar, carob powder or sesame seeds, as desired.

Dough can be stored 4 or 5 days in the refrigerator before frying.

. . . Among the major factors that led to a substantial improvement in the entire nutritional program in the twenty-seven mental hospitals of New York State was the introduction of special inexpensive foods of high nutritive value such as soy flour and dry skim milk into the dietary. In the course of two years the use of dry skim milk and soy flour were each increased by more than a million pounds annually.—C.M.M.

. . . Whole wheat flour probably contains nutrients such as vitamins in proper ratios that have been balanced by assimilation into the living plant.—C.M.M.

. . . Breads can serve as foods that are nearly complete if they are supplemented with calcium-rich skim milk, protein-rich soy flour, vitamin-rich nutritional yeast and wheat germ.—C.M.M.

Cornell Sourdough Breads

If you want to branch out from the ordinary, it's fun to play with starters, sponges and sourdoughs. These breads are tasty indeed.

The idea is to make up a soft mixture of water, yeast and flour and let it stand to ferment for several hours, overnight or even several days. This develops a yeasty flavor which many people especially like. The sourdough breads are delicious with cheese, cold cuts and flavorful meats such as ham, corned beef and tongue. They are a pleasant change from the usual daily bread.

Perhaps they appeal to our primitive instincts, because this is the way that the process of bread making probably developed—yeasts from the air, falling on moist flour, causing it to ferment and to become light when baked.

We have all heard of the sourdoughs of the western prospectors and the early homesteaders—the sponge or "starter" of the sourdough going on for months or even years. Some is taken out for baking, then more flour and water are added to the remains to be saved for the next time. However, if you are not making sourdough bread regularly, it is just as well to use it up soon and to start with a fresh batch for the next time.

. . . Gardening, baking and the processing of foods afford interesting hobbies and one of the best means of insuring the freshest foods for the older person.—C.M.M.

Sourdough "White"

To make the starter, PLACE in a bowl:
  2 cups warm water (105° to 115° F.)
  1 package active dry yeast
  2 cups unbleached flour
MIX together and let stand in a warm place overnight. If more flavor is desired, let stand for two or three days at room temperature. Stir at intervals.
PLACE in a large bowl when ready to make the bread:
  2 cups warm water (105° to 115° F.)
  1 package active dry yeast
LET STAND for 5 minutes.
STIR and BLEND in:
  1½ cups starter
  2 tablespoons honey or brown sugar
  2 tablespoons salad oil
  3 teaspoons sea salt
  3 tablespoons wheat germ
  ½ cup full-fat soy flour
  ¾ cup nonfat dry milk
  5 to 6 cups unbleached flour (part may be bran or whole wheat)
WORK and MIX flour in thoroughly and vigorously.
TURN dough onto floured board, using more flour if needed.

Figure 43. An appetizing assortment of sourdough loaves and rolls.

Figure 44. These starters for "white," rye and whole wheat sourdough breads have been standing all night.

KNEAD until dough is smooth and elastic.
PLACE in oiled bowl. Grease top of dough lightly and cover.
LET RISE in a warm place until nearly double in size.
PUNCH dough down and let rest while you prepare the pans.
SHAPE into 3 loaves.
LET RISE in pans and BAKE in a moderate oven, 350° F., until brown and loaves sound hollow when tapped.
REMOVE from pans and cool on rack.

For later baking, carry over the starter. To replenish add 1 cup more each of flour and warm water and 1 teaspoon sugar. Mix well, cover and keep in a warm place if it is to be used soon. Otherwise, put in the refrigerator.

The sourdough breads may be used in all the ways that the Cornell basic mix can appear—loaves, hamburger buns, with sprouts, etc. Sourdough *pitas* are especially good.

Sourdough Whole Wheat

[makes 2 loaves]

To make the whole wheat starter, PLACE in a large bowl:
    2 cups warm water (105° to 115° F.)

1 package active dry yeast
2 cups whole wheat flour
MIX together and let stand in a warm room overnight. If more flavor is desired, let it stand for two or three days at room temperature. Stir at intervals.
PLACE in a large mixing bowl and BLEND:
    ¼ cup warm water
    1 package active dry yeast
    2 cups whole wheat starter
    2 tablespoons wheat germ
    ¼ cup full-fat soy flour
    ⅓ cup nonfat dry milk
    ¼ cup dark molasses
    1 tablespoon sea salt
    3 tablespoons salad oil
BEAT IN gradually:
    2 to 3 cups unbleached flour
TURN dough onto board, using more flour if needed.
KNEAD vigorously about 5 minutes, until dough is smooth and elastic.
PLACE in an oiled bowl. Grease top of dough lightly and cover with plastic.
LET RISE in a warm place until double in size, an hour or more.
TURN onto board and divide into 2 portions. Let rest while you oil the baking pans. I put one portion in a loaf pan, 8 x 4½ x 3 inches, and braid the other to bake onto a sheet.
LET RISE to double in size, about an hour.
BAKE in a moderate oven, 350° F., for about 40 minutes, until loaves sound hollow when tapped.
REMOVE from pans and put on rack to cool.

Sourdough Rye

[makes 3 long slender loaves or 2 loaves and 10 rolls]

To make the starter, PLACE in a large bowl:
    2 cups warm water (105° to 115° F.)
    1 package active dry yeast
    2 cups rye flour
MIX together and let stand in a warm room overnight. If more flavor is desired, let stand for 2 or 3 days at room temperature. Stir at intervals.
PLACE in large mixing bowl:
    1 cup warm water (105° to 115° F.)
    1 package active dry yeast
STIR and BLEND IN:
    1½ cups rye starter
    ¼ cup dark molasses
    2 tablespoons caraway seeds
    1 egg
    1 tablespoon sea salt
    1 to 2 cups rye flour
    3 tablespoons salad oil
    3 tablespoons wheat germ
    ½ cup full-fat soy flour
    ¾ cup nonfat dry milk
BEAT IN gradually:
    3 to 4 cups unbleached flour
TURN dough onto floured board, using more flour if needed.

Figure 45. A braid and a loaf of sourdough whole wheat are ready to bake.

Figure 46. Loaves of sourdough rye ready to bake.

KNEAD vigorously about 5 minutes, until dough is smooth and elastic.

PLACE in an oiled bowl. Grease top of dough lightly and cover.

LET RISE in a warm place until nearly double, about 1 hour.

TURN onto board and divide into three portions. LET REST while you sprinkle cornmeal on a baking sheet.

FORM dough into long, narrow rolls and place to rise on pan, about an hour, until double in size.

CUT diagonal slashes on the top of each loaf with a sharp knife or razor.

BAKE in a moderate oven, 350° to 375° F., till crusty and brown and loaves sound hollow when tapped.

REMOVE from pan and cool on rack.

Sourdough Silver Dollar Pancakes

[serves 2 persons]

The whole wheat starter or, in fact, any of the sourdoughs, may be included in any bread recipe to give a delicious flavor. Simply adjust your recipe by adding a little more flour to give the right consistency to the dough.

Figure 47. Cornell waffles—a breakfast treat that's good for you too!

These sourdough sponges or starters make delicious pancakes and waffles.

PLACE in measuring cup:
   1 tablespoon full-fat soy flour
   1 tablespoon nonfat dry milk
   1 teaspoon wheat germ

FILL rest of cup with unbleached flour and ADD to 1 cup of starter (white, whole wheat or rye):
   1 egg
   ½ cup water
   ½ teaspoon sea salt
   1 tablespoon salad oil or bacon grease (if desired)
   1 teaspoon honey or molasses

STIR with an egg beater and LET STAND for 10 or 15 minutes while you are preparing rest of the breakfast.

DROP by spoonfuls onto a hot, greased griddle and serve at once.

Sourdough Waffles

[makes 4 waffles]

PLACE in mixing bowl and MIX:
   1 cup warm water (105° to 115° F.)
   1 package active dry yeast
   2 cups sourdough starter, which has ripened overnight or longer (either white, whole wheat or rye)
   1 tablespoon honey
   ½ cup salad oil
   1 teaspoon sea salt

LET STAND while you MEASURE into another bowl:
   2 tablespoons wheat germ
   ¼ cup full-fat soy flour
   ⅓ cup nonfat dry milk
   2 tablespoons sesame seeds (if desired)
   1½ cups unbleached flour (part can be whole wheat, buckwheat, etc.)

STIR the dry ingredients into the liquid ingredients with a spoon.

SEPARATE 2 large eggs. BEAT whites and yolks separately. STIR in yolks and lightly FOLD IN whites.

SET batter aside to rise for an hour or more.

BAKE on a hot waffle iron until waffles are crisp and brown.

Cornell Formula for the Bakery

Large Bakery Recipe

[straight-dough method; makes 200 loaves]

First to make the Cornell bread for large groups was the New York State Department of Mental Hygiene, Albany, New York, under the direction of Mrs. Katherine E. Flack, Director of Institution Services. This pioneer work to improve the diets of some one hundred thousand patients in the state's mental hospitals was a cooperative venture of Mrs. Flack, Cornell, and Mr. John Silva of the Dry Milk Institute.

Mrs. Flack recently reported the good news that the original Cornell formula is still being baked today in New York mental hospitals, as it has been these last twenty years. This is a marvellous record and a great compliment to Mrs. Flack and to all who helped to bring it about.

Here is the formula used by the bakers of the Department of Mental Hygiene in New York State:

100 pounds Northwest unbleached flour
72 (approximately) pounds water
2 pounds yeast
2 pounds salt
4 ounces yeast food
1 to 2 pounds sugar
1 pound malt (non-diastatic)
2 pounds shortening
8 pounds nonfat dry milk
6 pounds full-fat soy flour
2 pounds wheat germ

METHOD: It is important that the dough be properly mixed. It should be mixed enough to incorporate the ingredients together properly to secure a smooth dough. The mixing period depends on the type and speed of the mixer. The nonfat dry milk as well as the soy flour and wheat germ should be added on top of the flour and the mixing continued until the dough is dry and pliable.

TEMPERATURE: This depends largely on the temperature of the dough room. The most suitable temperature is 78° to 80° F. With normal water conditions, doughs should be set so that when fully matured and ready to go to the bench or divider they will have a temperature ranging between 81° and 82° F. Therefore, the dough should be delivered from the mixing machine at a temperature which will result in the proper temperature at the time of its maturity. Generally, this means that the dough is set so that directly after mixing it will have a temperature between 78° and 79° F.

FERMENTATION: After mixing, allow dough to rise until it is light enough so that it will recede if the hand is inserted and quickly withdrawn. Turn dough by pulling the ends and sides well in, and allow it to rest for 30 minutes. Turn again and take to bench or divider in 15 minutes.

PROOFING: During pan proof, too much moisture should not be applied to doughs containing high percentages of nonfat dry milk. If too much moisture is present the resulting crust will be somewhat tough and will have a foxy red color. It is also good to give this dough a little less proof before going to the oven. When this dough is properly mixed and fermented it will have a very good oven spring. Temperature of proof box should be around 90° to 94° F. with enough humidity so the loaves will not form a crust.

BAKING: If the sugar and malt contents are properly adjusted the baking temperature and time will be about the same as for regular bread. This type of bread, because of the high percentage of nonfat dry milk as well as soy flour, will color more quickly in the oven than will milk-free bread. The temperature of the oven should be such that the loaves will start to color in about 10 to 12 minutes after being placed in the oven. This type bread should be baked at 400° to 440° F. flash heat. Temporary excessive oven temperature at the start should be avoided inasmuch as it will cause a rapid crust formation and color too deeply. Underbaked bread will have an aroma suggestive of greenness, the texture will be over-moist and it will not slice and wrap well.

. . . We have been working for many years on the problem of maintaining bones and teeth in old age. From the number of broken hips and broken vertebrae, I have come to realize how important this is for hundreds of people. We have fed animals for their whole lives upon test diets, and then studied their bones and teeth after death . . . The best teeth we have seen are in animals that have had milk throughout the whole of life. In fact, the only teeth that we have ever seen that are not decayed in old age are the teeth of our experimental animals that have been fed on a liberal milk diet.—C.M.M.

. . . No evidence from our study indicates that milk will lead to any special disease such as hardening of the arteries or cancer.—C.M.M.

. . . The lack of information is not the problem in nutrition today. The vital blocks are a disinterest in learning, lack of self-discipline in food selection and the failure to realize that what one eats affects his health.—C.M.M.

. . . Older people need to reduce their consumption of sugar but when they use sweetening they will find brown sugar and dark molasses to contain some essentials such as iron.—C.M.M.

Small Bakery Recipe

[makes 25 loaves]

The following is a formula for a small bakery based on the one used by Mrs. Flack's bakers. This was baked for me by Gwaltney's Pastry Shop in Englewood, Florida. It can easily be used by camps, school lunches, restaurants and other health-conscious groups. Take this formula to your favorite baker. Persuade others to join in calling for the Cornell loaf so that you too can obtain good bread in your community.

8 pounds warm water
12½ pounds unbleached Northwest or gluten flour
12 ounces yeast
4 ounces sea salt
4 ounces sugar
4 ounces shortening
1 pound nonfat dry milk
3 ounces honey
3 ounces molasses
12 ounces full-fat soy flour
4 ounces wheat germ

METHOD: Put water in bowl first. Scale ingredients and add to water. Mix in first speed on a 3-speed mixer. Mix from 12 to 15 minutes. This dough must pull away from bowl. If not, add more flour so it will not be sticky.

TEMPERATURE: This depends on the temperature of the shop. Keep the dough covered with a cloth so it won't crust over. Mixing temperature is 78° to 80° F. Keep the temperature on the dough bench, 82° to 85° F.

FERMENTATION: After mixing allow dough to rise 20 to 30 minutes. Then divide into 1-pound loaves. Let rise about 20 minutes. Then put in bread pans.

PROOFING: Put in proof box with temperature about 90° to 94° F. for 20 to 30 minutes, or until bread is at top of pans.

BAKING: Bake in oven at 400° F. for 20 to 25 minutes. Take from oven and wash with shortening.

Any baker may make the Cornell formula without permission and without charge. However, each baker is requested to print the formula on the wrappers, including *how much* of each ingredient. Anyone can print "milk" on his label, but who knows whether it is a pinch or pound?

The label on Cornell bread should read that for every 100 parts of unbleached flour there are:

2 parts wheat germ
6 parts full-fat soy flour
8 parts nonfat dry milk

If you find these proportions on the wrapper, you'll know that you have Cornell bread.

. . . Rats were kept until they died of old age. The results were thoroughly tested, but anyone seeing the rats at the age of one year, or half-way through their span of life, would have noticed the difference immediately. Those fed the poor bread were sickly and most of them died young. These results indicate that one had better choose either the best bread available or eat more potatoes.

. . . The nutritional status of every person lies largely in his own hands during the latter half of life and depends largely upon his ability to curb his intake of such common foods as sugar, alcohol, low-grade cereals and many fats, as well as his ability to select foods of high nutritional value.—C.M.M.

. . . To get better bread, plus other baked goods and cake mixes as well, the goal of every housewife should be to insist on an "Open Formula"—a formula upon every package telling the exact amount of ingredients and the name and amount of any special chemicals used in the product.—C.M.M.

. . . This bread was baked by a new principle that had not been tried previously as far as we were aware. The formula of the bread was printed on the wrapper.—C.M.M.

Heroes in the Laboratory

Here are representatives of two large groups of experimental animals. They are the same ages, but Cornell bread has given the first one health and the power to grow, while the little one who ate ordinary bread, was unable to grow and soon died.

A booklet about Cornell bread would not be complete without this photo that tells the story of many repeated experiments at Cornell. It shows how the protein of dry milk and soy flour can bring the missing amino acids to wheat so that animals can live in health on bread and butter and reproduce successfully. Because these little heroes and man have similar nutritional needs, what's good for them is usually good for us.

Clive made many studies to learn how far the life span of the white rat could be stretched by a careful selection of high-quality foods. Here is his conclusion:

. . . The best method we have discovered for retarding the onset of old-age diseases is to keep animals thin upon a modest allowance of a diet more than adequate in foods rich in vitamins, minerals and proteins.—C.M.M.

Figure 48. These little fellows are both the same age—but the one on the left has been fed on Cornell bread, while his friend was given ordinary bread.